I WANT TO WRITE AN HONEST SENTENCE

15 Sept 19

for John —
in New Haven, and hoping
for Hawaii —

w/ aloha,
Luc

also by Susan M. Schultz

Poetry

Aleatory Allegories, Salt, 2000
Memory Cards & Adoption Papers, Potes & Poets, 2001
And Then Something Happened, Salt, 2004
Dementia Blog, Singing Horse Press, 2008
Memory Cards: 2010-2011 Series, Singing Horse Press, 2011
"She's Welcome to Her Disease": Dementia Blog, Vol. 2,
Singing Horse Press, 2013
Memory Cards: Dogen Series, Vagabond Press, 2014
Memory Cards: Thomas Traherne Series, Talisman House, 2016
Memory Cards: Simone Weil Series, Equipage Press, 2017

Criticism

*A Poetics of Impasse in Modern and Contemporary American
Poetry*, Alabama, 2005
The Tribe of John: Ashbery and Contemporary Poetry, editor,
Alabama, 1995
Multiformalisms: Postmodern Poetics of Form, editor with Annie
Finch, Word Press, 2009

I WANT TO WRITE AN HONEST SENTENCE

SUSAN M. SCHULTZ

Talisman House, Publishers
Northfield, Massachusetts • 2019

Published in the United States of America by
Talisman House Publishers
PO Box 102
Northfield, MA 01360

Manufactured in the United States of America

11 12 13 7 6 5 4 3 2 1

ISBN: 978-1-58498-136-7

ACKNOWLEDGMENTS
Thank you to Anselm Berrigan (*Brooklyn Rail*), Eileen Tabios (*Galatea Resurrects, Marsh Hawk Review*), Ed Foster (*Talisman*), Lou Rowan (*Golden Handcuffs*), and John Bloomberg-Rissman (*End of the World*) for publishing poems included in this book. Thanks also to Tommy Hite for his honest painting and to Gaye Chan for putting us in touch.

Much gratitude to the late Marthe Reed, Mike Kalish, and Laura Mullen (you know), as well as Tim Dyke in Honolulu and Caroline Garrett in Volcano.

To everyone who is resisting American fascism.

In memoriam Paul Lyons, Monica Brzezinski Potkay, Marthe Reed, Dennis Kosanke, Harold Anderson.

With love to Bryant, Sangha, Radhika, for your courage and for trusting me with some of your stories. Thank you to Lilith for many walks, and to Thurney and Maeve for being such cats.

IN MEMORY OF MY FATHER,
FREDERICK W. SCHULTZ (1913-1992)

I WANT TO WRITE AN HONEST SENTENCE

I want to write an honest sentence, one as true as the weather. But nothing's so untrue as weather, forgettable as pain on the Koʻolau's windward side. The mountain's obscure, it cannot be read. It blocks every attempt, calls back the occasional hiker. They searched for months for a boy in slippers. Don't trust a liar when he tells you the news is #Fake, even if his platform is suitable to the lyric. Threads unspool like couplets. He said his lips were seals, and our daughter didn't get it. She's got humor deficiency disorder (HDD). Thought Romeo tore his trousers on the balcony; I told her he hid his erection. Only some bodies are bawdy. In his late poems there's either the performance of senility or senility itself. My mother's friend's daughter wouldn't recognize her uncle, though she might see her son in his early photos. Baby thrust out on a father's arm; precarity's joy. Divorced from late capital, that is. I can't remember the weather, though I think it was too hot last summer, and rainy. Gray clouds have passed and now the sky is white. Somewhere in the alphabet, Ron told me, there's a section about the weather. Did he express feeling? someone asked. Attention cannot but involve feeling, a sense that something exists on the lawn apart from us, toad or lizard or the dog shit someone couldn't find to throw away. Car alarm and rustling trees, digital music pulse, my daughter's voice. Even the abstract can be attended to. I understand none of them; they are like the mountains or the avant-garde. Helicopter clutter, some doves. What I wrote two years ago I failed to remember, and yet it made sense. The vocabulary of politics without the politics. That's not true or fake, is presumptive. To appropriate is not to make a statement, but to till the earth for one. Only the pure survive, staring in mirrors like weightlifters to see that their posture is true. I've chosen the elliptical, it's so like running on an ostrich egg. On the screen a poker game, commentary I can't hear. The son's lawyer was paid by the president's campaign, before the act in question. "That was before the Russia carnival started!" he says, who is its prime barker. This weekend our populist plays golf. Real golf.

~16 July 2017

1

I want to write an honest sentence. I want to write a sentence I can own, not in the way I own objects but how I take responsibility for the air inside my room, breathing as a form of attention that enters without staying. Nothing stays, though "it stay hot" denotes a change of condition. He who cannot own his failure tries for a better one, destruction without hope of renovation, a blackened high rise to remind us there's more to life than structure. Strictures bind us to our dog, who is pet inside the house and animal outside. Nasal appraisal, one neighbor calls it, nose to the grass, a way of reading in no particular direction, though leaves require particular energies to decipher. A swift intake of breath is not grammar or syntax, less an unfolding than a claim on the air that's instantly repaid. Her nose on my arm tickles, a greeting that is also inventory. Palm fronds shield us from the asphalt ribbon they put down on our field, the better to protect their golf carts from injury. A two cart parking lot adorns the front of the ever-growing shed. Cart Path Project, it's called. Black ribbon on a green field, no Barnett Newman that. Stations have not opened, though concrete ribbons run across the Leeward side. Look at the earth, my father would say, its rich reds or clays. I took to looking up instead, but age pulls us down a peg, pushes our eyeballs into what's left of the commons, pulls up fences like blue tape. The blue whale game, while horrifying, may prove to be a hoax. The girl painted blue whales, but her family had no idea she spoke Russian. Each one cuts a blade in our emotional skin, leaving a ribbon of blood behind our eyes. The Senator's surgery was more complicated than had been thought, so he couldn't get to DC in time to vote against others' health care. Irony prevention is what we need, with small co-pays. She teaches irony by showing her students a bus marked by a huge sign advertising safety, a bus that has just run into a car. The car resembles a crushed maroon paper flower, or the sculptured trash can a president throws his deed inside. "I will not own this," he says; he only owns what he destroys, the negative space charcoal is good at getting at. My daughter learned perspective last week; this week she's on to ceramics and soccer. I haven't seen monks play, but her passes sometimes defy physics. Space is time that's been thrown on a wheel.

~18 July 2017

2

I want to write an honest sentence. A myna waves blue Dorito bag like a flag across Hui Iwa. Simile as false flag. Not the sound of a flag, its appearance in the beak of a brown and black bird. The sentence is true, if not honest. In that micro-difference we parse an older politics, the seen but not spoken hijinks of wink. There was hidden meaning, so we felt we were reading poems and there was some value in learning how to analyze a text. What was hidden has now floated to the top like crude, and it is. He wants to stay in the Senate, doesn't he? The aesthetics of a threat is pretty lame. I want my daughter to feel the joy of having her pass pushed toward the goal; an angle makes the run true. I also want her to drink clear water until she dies. Bryant nearly cried when he told her that she would die. Existence is value that cannot be laundered, like a casino or tower. My son stands in front of an unnamed castle in Naples. Where ancient and modern rub together, my glasses need replacement. Stigmata or astigmatism. We no longer read his work for meaning, but for lexicons spread upon the plate, platitudes exhumed and replaced in reverse order. Where were the September towers, the airport warriors, flags plastered on walls? Adept of attention, he paid none. It cost too much. The massacre at Mosul takes place outside our camera lens. Even within it, there's nothing to see. Nothing to see in secret meetings without aides or translators. Nothing to see. My dog's brown and black ears frame an ocean that's still blue. Even if the blue whale game is false, young women still kill themselves. The new comfort is found in everything fake. After he confessed to the crime, his supporters still thought the news was false. The fake of a fake is still fake, until in this long wall of mirrors laws of diminishment reduce us to dots, like distant seals in a cold sea. That word looks true, but a wavering red line appears beneath it. Red sea spelling bad. She smelled Sewer View Gardens but placed it on the wrong side of the street. Eye exams depend on solitary letters. Even as my vision coheres, there's no meaning, just ever tinier lines to decipher. You're a good guesser, she said, and I felt like Bengie Molina catching 90 mph pitches in the Puerto Rican dark. When you can't see them otherwise, you get good at spotting pitches as they leave the pitcher's hand.

~19 July 2017

3

I want to write an honest sentence. *This is not normal* would be one. Academic mobbing is a thing; you can chart it by seeing how colleagues walk the corridors. One wears Beats and dances past. Another leaves the elevator, device planted in front of face like a palm. "Are you gossiping again?" my daughter asks and I explain that gossip is how women warn each other; it's a micro-politics that is suddenly out-sized. If he'd told me he'd recuse himself, I'd never have hired him. The individual is one thing, the all-consuming sponge another. I read Ponge as a freshman, loved and then forgot him. And now I'm trapped inside the chaos theory surface of a public ego. He really liked to hold my hand, he said three times in a row. Row row row your boat works as zen wisdom. My mother rowed into the Bay of Naples to be alone, but a soldier rented a boat to keep her company. Her story repeated so many times it became a round in my head. I don't remember if it's in the video the neighbor made of her telling stories, the neighbor who's in prison for sexual battery of a minor. Undercurrents, riptides. A chain of 80 people formed from shore to the swimmers in distress. That was the good news last week. They doth accumulate, his lies, piles of sand in an hourglass. The video of my mother now matters as much for audio of the neighbor, his inquiring voice, his fondling of her memory. Spool! Banana peels on a south London stage. Words make old technology sexy. If I had audio of that meeting, I'd put it in the closet with my mother's ashes. Don't bring up the past, they said. Don't you know students act that way? Feather in our cap, but. The drawer closed, as did my door. His poems are full of them, but they're usually ajar. Inoculation against assumptions, no anti-vaxxer I. Her photos of my son and his friend were done in fish-eye, though time warped the rest. I see he saw my message, but I get no message back. It's like responding to Trump's tweets; the glory is in doing it. But that's a distraction! The woman with the Big Gulp fed her granddaughter a spam musubi, rice clump by rice grain. She drives a pink electric car and says "true love!" at bed-time. It's Disney, you know. The French theorist had nothing on us now. You should see the refugees' ride.

--20 July 2017

4

I want to write an honest sentence. I want to write that experiments are the new realism, that they must be conscious, even if their subjects are not. The Alzheimer's home a colony, run by a bureaucracy of outsiders, its rules unreadable to the residents. Land and rent its raw materials. A cure for memory's lacerations, this band of crickets, birds, helicopters, my husband scraping the wood stove. "They're so beautiful," she said of the same flowers, over and again. The red spotted orchid's a double-decker, petal laid lightly over petal. The next day it's shrunk to a red point on a green stalk. On Haunani Road, an Asian man stops his truck and gets out. There's a handicapped sticker on his mirror, and his legs are bent oddly, painfully, out. "There's a sign up the road," he tells me, "to say they're going to subdivide five acres into 12 lots and build houses." And those cars! Abandoned, rusted, sinking in front of an empty house. "The community should have a say," he tells me, before getting back in his truck. I find the sign, cloaked by vines, date it back to 2010, hope it's been forgotten, or papers misplaced, and then turn off Haunani onto a gravel road toward Wright. Development is forgetting by way of accumulation. First you scrape the rain forest off the lot, then you let it sit, a few trunks upright in the dark earth. To remember is to love the material world, to add to it. Consider that there's ambition in forgetting, even in being forgotten. He was so resistant to attention, Miho says of Saijo, that no one's heard of him. Only a bit player in that movie, sick man in a hospital who watches his healthy Beat friends light out for the territories. To be forgotten is perhaps the greatest blessing, but he cannot ask his friends to abandon the picture of him by his stove, talking always talking about empire, corruption and the blessings of pot. To be abandoned is not the worst of it. There used to be i'iwi's on I'iwi Road, but they fled to Mauna Loa when mosquitoes arrived. The only i'iwi you see here is a dead i'iwi. They sound like rusty hinges, opening and closing in the forest canopy. I took a picture of a gate on Laukapu Road whose post was more rust than iron. Lace is an old lady's hobby, she was told. But red lace in a rain forest forgets its category and dissolves.

--1 August 2017

I want to write an honest sentence that is not like the others. Form to follow function requires me to better think about function. The newest experiment is spare record of water drops on broad leaves. Too much detail denotes trauma, too little the same. Repeat signs were emojis before the fact. "There there" or "the the" finds laughter in repetition. An old Cambodian woman asked for more gruel and was killed in front of our friend. My students could not forgive him his laughter. They wouldn't stop bringing it up. Our friend gave them his trauma and they blamed him for it. I wonder how they remember him from their late 20s or early 30s, driving to work, feeding their kids, mowing their lawns. Only later did I see it as a kind of generosity of spirit, his offering of story. Later iterations of his were softer, until trauma seemed to have bled out and we'd arrived at a horrible going–to–camp narrative that didn't jar us from our desks. Most American workers have suffered the trauma of bullying or mobbing in their jobs; psychologists need to understand the phenomenon of ganging up on scapegoats and forcing them out of work. Jeff Sessions oddly knows this, the racist bully. Administration, typically, sides with the mob; most others remain silent and are traumatized in their turn by what they witness. The survivor is scarred, but at his best sanctified by this experience. Saints don't get much health insurance, however, or tuition money for their kids. You've gotta be in the 1% to express your empathy, but once you're there, you've got your eyes on a different prize. This morning birds punctuate the forest with song. A distant bulldozer diminishes their surround. When I asked students to give examples of systems, one said "buddy." Beside the road a layer of rock holds up a layer of soil. It's thinner than you might think, spongy with dead hapu'u fronds. If you don't learn the names, they'll all disappear. If you do, sing them in rounds. Spread the trauma of repeated sound.

--2 August 2017

I want to write an honest sentence about career, about the way I can't write an honest sentence about career. It's a stand-in word like a hat rack, denoting motivation and—always—hypocrisy. I may have volition, but my desires are never pure. If I'm with you 80% that makes me more dangerous than if I'm only with you for a dash through the park with my dog; her name hearkens back to demons and early feminists but can't be found in Genesis. To say you're an "ally" is an act of aggression, reads one thread. To be an older woman is to be not-seen; to be a young man is to see oneself too clearly as deficient. Have you ever seen Trump play with his boy? The fault of parenting is most of it. I try to stand on the other side of the white fence, wearing my break-away collar so as not to break my neck, but there's no letting go, exactly. When I sat next to her at the Corcoran, I could feel my substance being sucked into hers, the pain of it. Take inventory of your family's traumas. They pale before the Khmer Rouge, though that's in there somewhere, too. Pale or no, we deal with what we're given (no gift). There's an aura around things in one's late 30s, Ashbery notes, but by the late 50s, there's an absence inside of everything, an ache like the hapu'u fern that fills a rain forest but leaves holes for the light. It's the Holier Than Thou School of Poetry, setting one poet on the top of her pedestal, inventing her motivations whole cloth, the better to knock her down like Saddam. The shroud of Turin bore only one silhouette, but these are ghosted by the stain of our desire for attention. Not the attention we devote to bird song but to ourselves. He tried to fake himself out in the mirror before he knew who he was. That wasn't Narcissism but self-discovery. He gave his son his false name, the one he called radio stations with to defend his primary self, the one with the name we know him by. My son's name denotes community, but also means he's handsome. We wear the same baseball caps; they denote an identity we can traverse without real pain.

—6 August 2017

7

I want to write an honest sentence about the white man at the gym. I on my elliptical and he on his stationary bike, while above us Rachel Maddow preaches in closed captions. I keep my eye on him and on the captions until—out of nowhere, it seems to me—he yells "PIG!" while maintaining his unmoving stride. He's often here, in Green Bay cap, peddling off (or on) his fire and fury, telling the woman who sneaks a peek at Maddow that she's a "socialist fool." I want to ask if he's ok, but imagine he punches me in the face, gets thrown out. There's hate on many sides, Trump tells us today, after a car plows into a Charlottesville crowd, killing one woman, injuring those to whom he sends his "best regards." The young men in the video are handsome, in casual slacks grasping tiki torches. Perhaps they go to a gym in Ohio or Alabama or Charlottesville to make themselves pretty for the cameras. No hoods, no robes. Just those damn tiki torches like our neighbors have on their lanai. The Dodge Challenger's front bumper destroyed, it sits stationary in an intersection near Fort Street Mall. The woman who was killed, I read, was simply crossing the street. At a small diner in Williamsburg a white couple grumbled that a black woman hadn't smiled at them. She left with her daughter; they skipped down the street, the one holding a bag, the other in pig tails. She hadn't been there to serve them. I mumbled an apology to the waitress. "You noticed, did you?" she said. Red brick serpentine walls blocked us from gardens near the lawn. I sat on a young man's lap in one garden, kissing. There's no accounting for emotional flooding; it means so little. In Kathmandu, they ask if you want to visit the Jew (zoo). Today, men yelled, "Jew won't remove us." I'll hide in that sonnet with the remover to remove. The last president tweets about love. He's an outside agitator now.

~12 August 2017

I want to write an honest sentence. "I don't want to kill people, but I will if I have to." He's pulling guns off his body in a motel room in North Carolina as his computer screen cups a swastika to the camera. The pale white woman with large glasses asks him about the woman who was killed; he assures her that more will die. He speaks in dead logic, noun verb object, always an object of scorn. Animals. He says he misplaced a second AK-47 for a moment: "imagine that!" Gun grammar employs active voice, even when it's silent, wrapped around its owner like a mink stole. On a walk with my bright blue Schwinn, my father pulled me off the sidewalk into some trees. The police had gone into the woods on the other side where an empty car was parked. Just in case. Just in case someone should get angry and drive to the mall. Just in case someone had been radicalized by his faith. Just in case we were walking down that narrow brick-lined street at the wrong time. Just in case the car was weaponized. The woman with wide open eyes was killed; I want her eyes but not her end. To the martyr go no relics save some iPhone video, a couple of photos, some flowers laid inside a heart near Water Street. You can sit with a relic. You can sing to it in frail voices, but you cannot rest within the instant gratification of grief. Which is his gun of choice, the long or the short, the one in his pants or the one strapped to his ankle? American murderers are good consumers, just like the rest of us. "The master looks down on us every day from his mountain," a black woman says. This is nothing new, it's just more visible. Identify this bearded white man, the one who beat up the after-school aide who pushes the swings so well. As fashion statement, hoods do better. My friend remembers turning a corner at UVA and finding himself face to face with the Dalai Lama. In the photo he appends, it's 5:11 p.m.; the Dalai Lama's right foot juts out in covered shoes. Almost the dandy, he holds his dark robe up. "He smiled and nodded."

--15 August 2017

9

I want to write an honest sentence about the effect of distraction on the long poem. Confusion was depression's door man, his gloved hands and silk hat waving across our line of sight like roads in old movies, so clearly spliced in. His wall eyes had everything to do with what we could not see. Neck tilted, he gazed at the rafters, then read a poem about a dashboard, or were they windshield wipers? Over time, the discursive stain deepened into word-image. Catch echoes like geckos until they die. When out of the late night's silence a chorus of roosters and a dog, a siren and spitting rain. Type cast, like paragraphs. I cast my fate with Fate Yanagi because someone loved her. There are words that mean something other than themselves, like leche, like faggot. When you write them on the board they last as image only. Once upon a time, the fossil poem got lost in amber and was never found. Once upon a time, we lost the meaning of such words as made our lives possible, words like "fragility" and "forgiveness." Or pathos, which no one leaves alone. Is piano hammers on the chest, damper to the throat. Is the odd violence of music during depression. Now that his meds have kicked in, he likes piano music. There's less to take in, but it's better received. You cannot wall out sound. When there's concrete to be poured, bury Harvey's drowned pianos in it like Jimmy Hoffa at the Meadowlands. For music is an immigrant, legal or not, that crosses deserts at night and beds down beside the cactus. Or sleeps to die in containers. He was acknowledged, but cannot legislate our escape. Nor can we, ears to the tracks, praying for the distant clacking of those keys. Remember that borders became boarders (footnote, John Shoptaw), that the wall was a giant well we threw our pennies in. They're living on our dime, she said of the homeless, and we can't even afford the house we live in. They take our dollars for drugs. You might need them, too, Bryant responded, if you were sick and on the street. Her husband stopped the conversation. You cannot persuade each other, he said. And so we turned our attention to Portuguese water dogs, who leapt in the pool after orange rubber balls. Their joy salved something.

--4 September 2017

I want to write an honest sentence, one without judgment. When young, we're reaction machines—like the student who leaped in the air when I called his name—but then a long slow distancing begins. We acquire a moat, or see-through border wall, between us and our emotions. My response to the death of a poet is to imitate his sentences like Matt Morris throwing Darryl Kile's curve two days after Kile died. Style's a form of grieving, one that threads out like a shawl over bent shoulders. We see weight in the absence of uplift. Or in a back's bony protrusions. Occasionally, I see an old Asian woman doubled over at the waist, walking intently across a street. We interpret that angle as hard work or as hard emotion or as osteoperosis. I asked my students to define "haole" and to use the word in a sentence, which they did with utmost accuracy. Even within the context of bad history, it stung to read their answers about how those who are pale as ghosts lack breath, are foreign, outside. The man explains to his child self why another boy hit him on the head with a 2' by 4' as if he were half a metronome. One student described this as an embarrassing moment, not for the bully but for the bullied. Perhaps his skull didn't keep good time. To revise is to take private thoughts and work them into public shape. The guys at the gym do this in front of mirrors that are at once for them and for us. The distortion is all in my seeing you seeing yourself (muscle bound) in a wall length piece of glass. The woman who asked me to deliver her divorce papers trusted a stranger to do the work of making her private grief public. "Don't ask how I got involved," I said as I turned back toward the gate, away from the yapping dogs and the smiling man. She was haole, he Hawaiian. "You live on an island" has so many meanings, not all of them geographical. But check your metaphors at the door; this is an age of literal fact and lie. His biographers, he says, have no access. That makes all of it fake news, as if "fake" were such a bad thing.

~12 September 2017

11

I want to write an honest sentence about exposition or, more accurately, about its lack. Interpretation is a kind of exposure, like the time I peered down from a cliff at a rocky pool and saw naked men and women sunning on the rocks. There was also the sad parrot that destroyed his perch by pecking at it. The sound interrupted our lunch, because nakedness requires an obstacle to interpret its lack of cover. Fashion statements are cover stories that we read over lunch, though I can't imagine hovering like a drone over any of my recent meals. A drone flew over us at the walk out of darkness, but drones don't kill themselves so the point was lost on me. Drone operators do, for reasons of alienation even from the killing that they do. Death in the age of Dilbert, cubicle after cubicle inhabited by office chair soldiers; I read that sitting kills us, so why not kill others while seated? Where do you find a cover story, when you never left your chair? John says I should add question marks to my exposition on exposition, but that would render too obvious the nakedness of my punctuation. After a bag blew up in the Tube, dear leader wrote about "terrorist losers." I'm surprised he didn't spell it "loosers," as losers seems to be loosening over time, adding another vowel to its slack elastic. John Lennon was a looser, but at least we could sing along as if not to think about ourselves but about him. My student who suffers from selective mutism says she likes to sing, but not in public. That would be too much exposition, self- or otherwise. I told my students that despite my hardened shell, seeing them write over and over that haoles "lack breath" and are "foreigners" started to hurt. The dull ache of being set apart. It's been a hard year, Radhika writes on Instagram, but there aren't enough words to explain. Her photograph seems divorced from any of that, exposure of a different kind, an orange sun rising over surfers, because—as she'd say—it's in the east. They seem to sit in the ocean, as if divorced from gravity or balance, watching everything that's coming up in its hunky glory.

--16 September 2017

I want to write an honest sentence about trauma, about a dent in the
   consuming rose.
I want to write an honest sentence about trauma, about my former student
   who asks if he's ok.
I want to write an honest sentence about trauma, about the way the P falls
   off the TSD.
I want to write an honest sentence about trauma, about how not making
   sense of it yet will last a lifetime.
I want to write an honest sentence about trauma, about how not sleeping
   is nightmare's discipline.
I want to write an honest sentence about trauma, the trauma-rama.
I want to write an honest sentence about trauma, how real in a false city.
I want to write an honest sentence about trauma, about my other former
   student who stayed 10 floors below that "monster."
I want to write an honest sentence about how trauma takes the roller
   coaster through New York New York.
I want to write an honest sentence about the heads that blew off before he
   decided to run.
I want to write an honest sentence about how he just needs xanax because
   he can't breathe.
I want to write an honest sentence about how none of us can breathe.
I want to write an honest sentence about the bad air.
I want to write an honest sentence about the president who picks up a roll
   of paper towels and tosses them into the crowd like a basketball after
   holding a can of tuna up to the cameras.
I want to write an honest sentence about 23 people crowded into a hotel
   room wondering who they are now.
I want to write an honest sentence that is not consumed by rage.
I want to write an honest sentence of compassion, not "this country is so
   fucked up," each hour on the hour.
I want to write an honest sentence about trauma, how it invites us into its
   hotel room and asks us to look out through the scopes at the still
   happy people.

for Nick Wilson
~3 October 2017

I want to write an honest sentence about control. After her dog lost control, she hosed her down for hours. There was also a tumor underneath her heart. We control crowds, not guns, birth not medical costs. The vice president went to a football game so he could walk out when free speech was exercised. The man who took the first knee says he'll stand to get his job back. And the homeless are so filthy in their ragged tents. They made their choices. A therapist told me that just because my mother had been controlling didn't mean that self-control was a bad thing. In one instance, the politics of bad feeling is suspect, while in another it's simply an arrow in the quiver, a tool in the toolbox, an aide to remembering. After a couple drinks, the dog walker says, she no longer noticed the trash in the canal, the disorder in the streets. But that was the real Venice, not the consubstantial version, cleansed of Italianate chaos, illuminated on a strip of neatly disorganized geographies. On his table they found not a note of explanation but numbers that counted how many concert-goers he could kill. My former student worries that he stepped on a dead person's hand. That he can't yet make sense of the event. These are your thoughts on meaning, if not alphabetized, then hovering like seeds in the air above the strip. There's none to be had; the house wins every time. Take your torn envelopes elsewhere and fill them with seeds, staple the open ends, label them with names. There's no purchase for them in a desert.

~8 October 2017

I want to write an honest sentence about ethics. After I read from *Dementia Blog, a* disability scholar inquired if I'd asked permission of my mother to write her story. (I had become my mother's keeper.) She asked if I had permission of the family. (There was none.) There's an ethics of privacy and there's one to counter it. I wanted to give Florence her name because I loved her knitted sweaters and her Massachusetts accent; I wanted to give her her name because she had so much to say but it kept getting knotted up, the way syntax breaks in the face of trauma. "Am I ok?" he kept asking. I wanted to know the name of his friend who'd died, but he couldn't type it. I'd pray anyway, in my funny way. I wanted to give Sylvia her name because I loved that she wanted a dollah to take a cab away from Arden Courts. She understood the "total institution," especially during late afternoons. Her son had to sneak away. These days I'm overtaken by mixed states—they call it "poignancy"—when the banana fruit opens and I see it from below, held up by a single wing, not yet fruit but a red globe beneath a jagged leaf. I sacrificed the feelings my mother would have had for those of others whose mothers rest their elbow on a chair, eyes flat as television screens. If you held her hand, she might feel better, though you'd never know. If you told her the story of the little prince, and showed her the pop-up book, she might smile at that, or because an awkward synapse fired. If you tried to find meaning, you might only find a mirror. When she looked in hers, she didn't see herself. Please, if I get there, call me by my name. It died out in 1966.

~13 October 2017

I want to write an honest sentence. Amar is 16 and lives in Mosul; he has just come out of the river, soaking wet. His parents were killed by ISIS, his younger sister paralyzed. Their uncle, with whom they live, does not feed or care for them. Amar sings about his mother to the journalist who asks him questions; the sweetness of his grief floods my car at rush hour. We're numb to what's happening, a student says; all that's left of the Vegas massacre is a large banner on the side of the Mandalay. Mandalas are for disappearing, but not the trauma we've outsourced to others. Fifty thousand Americans died of overdoses last year alone. Alone denotes a single year, not person. Their parents talk to us about addiction, about costs, about funding, because no matter where you start, you end with money. The young Hawaiian beside me told the story of "middle of nowhere" Oregon, where he'd been harassed by police. Asked what kind of Monster he drank, he laughed. They called in back-up. An hour and a half hassle for hitting a few inches of curb on the way into 7-11. "That wasn't a story, though you probably wanted it to be," said the Mexican kid in workshop. "That was an experience you were writing." His aunty told him he'd get dates because he's light-skinned. "No one wants to date a peasant," she said, and he wondered how to respond, so he didn't. What they left out of reader-response theory was what happens when there is none, when what we're told makes no sense, though it hurts. If you give me words to describe your rape, your mobbing, your curling in a ball on the bathroom floor, what am I to do with your gift? The girls of Boko Haram hide their faces behind hands and flowers. Men strapped bombs beneath their robes. The first abuses were precursors, foreplay to the rain of flesh and fabric that was to be their only inheritance. I love you, we say, I love you. The thick mesh of our monosyllables holds some of it back.

~27 October 2017

I want to write an honest sentence. Each clause begins, "In furtherance of their scheme," then concludes with what money was laundered where. Room after room disgorges its towels and sheets for Filipina maids to spirit away. But the scheme involves money, a lot of it, and off-shore accounts have nothing to do with reefs or wave patterns, rather with Company A and Company B, with carpets and Range Rovers, with condos and lawn services. Where every transaction is a cover story, there can be no depth. This ocean is flat as the stage set for an opera: two women on a boat lose their cell phone and disappear in the Pacific. Four months later they're found, funnily enough, alive. Not every sentence matters but they're all material, like the scarlet yarn that emerges from a chicken's entrails, turning butchery into narrative, as per always. To tell a story is to lose it like a lock or to hide beneath it. To pick the story is to indict its tellers, draw them out of their Virginia mansions. One taxi driver said houses had nothing in them, were shells set in the grass to impress the neighbors. The flag of our disposition is a deposition. Fake news is true insofar as someone calls it false, and false is true when it leads us down long corridors past room service and into the gunman's suite, now set off with police tape. He killed so many people because he didn't get into a good school. He killed them because his father was a psychopath. He killed them because his girlfriend was in the Philippines. He killed them because he killed them. What are these tender buttons but triggers we curl our fingers around, like a baby's hand our own. Tender is not the word, unless we consider the offer a good one. I pay my kids' tuition with the money I have taken from you. We will pull the lid off a bleached reef and watch it stare through the water's crust. No one to see the Range Rover, or the condo. He's driven off, face hidden by a sun visor, though one angle shows him smiling.

~31 October 2017

I want to write an honest sentence about the end of the world. It's coming, you know; how you feel about it matters less than what you do with your remaining sentences. You ransom them for more, or trade them at the deadline for a rental starter who can get you into the post-season, maybe earn you a title before the empty months stretch out with their rainy days and hot stove rumors. Working without a title can be liberating, like writing when you know that no one cares. The choreography of an academic department charts avoidance, curves away from and toward heavy brown doors that open onto drab clean pathways. I asked a young man if I could help; he said he was just looking around, then disappeared in thin air. In this political season, every encounter seems over-determined. The Proud Boys wear heavy black boots. My former student said one of them's a "nice guy." Niceness in an age of belligerence is no virtue. Is mask unto self or the cars that roar by between us. (He bought his Trump mask used.) The inevitable *verkehr* that we giggled over in class. It means "sexual intercourse," you know, along with "traffic." Why the heathens rage filled the newspapers of my youth. Now democracy dies in darkness. Deep as any dingle. I get my news on a feed, but what I learn is we're being fed a line, or two, grand epic of budget cuts. Whan that April with his slash and burn doth rid us of our literature, then we'll work as marketers of dreck. But back to the end of the world, which rises like the sun on our side of the island; it's on the other side that it falls, orange, over the earth's frail scalp. Nostalgia's the new revolution, an open square where citizens congregate and children kick balls. What we call terror they might have called poverty, but as my friend reminds me, the lotus comes from mud.

~5 November 2017

18

I want to write an honest sentence about kindness. The pastor used his motorcycle as a vehicle for allegory. He placed it in front of the altar, all buffed chrome and handlebars, then invited kids to sit on it. Their evening Bible study would be Revelations, and likely they'd not get past *I know thy works, that thou hast a name that thou livest, and art dead.* We're so in touch with our rage, so divorced from other affect. So firm in our faith that to pray can't stop a bullet, but can bless its aftermath of pain. It's as if 1.3 million New Yorkers had been killed. (The famous poet opened my documentary poetry class, "Poetry is the art form that does not include information.") Neither his palms nor ours are trees, more like grasses that bend away from trade winds and absorb the shock of baseball bats. Radhika says she broke a defender yesterday, meaning she split a post used to imitate one. Even grass shall lose its tenure in this United States of Fallacy. A hero neighbor stopped the slaughter at only 27; if he'd not had a gun to shoot the man with the gun, then everyone would've lain down on their fields and watered the ground with their blood, no questions asked. Earth is more fertile that way. Its roots and stalks take us at our words, but words grow mold, live their own disintegration. Our classrooms stink of it. Is there kindness to see how damaged we are that we kill but semi-automatically? Is there compassion enough to wrap these sick white men in blankets, pour soup down their ravening maws? *I will come on thee as a thief, and thou shalt not know what hour I will come upon thee.*

~7 November 2017

19

I want to write an honest sentence. It was a conference of clouds. Ash-bery's instruction manual foretold the cloud. A woman with small dog, no shoes, told me to distinguish healthy from unhealthy clouds. She counts them from the plane, though she uses no money and wears what she makes from what she finds at the transfer station. I hold the Ashbery po-em in my hand, but the man with the cloud keeps reading to me about heavy metals used to make iPhones. An unhealthy cloud is dark, but brings no rain. Her father, I find out, was the Hat Man of Maui. Broad smile, very few teeth. He'd played for the New England Patriots. When I leave, I see her again, leading her tan and white dog. No one came to her panel. The man with the cloud wore multi-colored slippers under his tight rolled up pants. I watched them under the table as he read to us, lifting each printed page across as he started to read it. My head was in the clouds, though I kept trying to land, aware the final approach might push me back in the air of this room with no access to Apple TV and only a wall on which to project what might have been given. Later, I open the im-age of a young woman on my computer; I didn't know her but recognize her face. She died in August. We cannot grieve if we lock our cloud against the air. It's dark, but cannot cry with us; instead, our faces swell and we cough as if to transfer affect into substance. That's what I was saying, he told me, that what we think is abstract never is.

-11 November 2017

I want to write an honest sentence. Someone asks what it's called when you keep starting over in the same way. Surely there's a name for this, other than obsession or compulsion or a strange insistence. We tell those stories that make us feel better, and this is mine. Once upon a time, the word "fragility" meant we weren't to drop a box, or push a glass off the counter top. After leaving the station of fact, our word wandered into a courtroom. A lawyer argued that she was easily broken, that he couldn't handle being questioned, that they denied the privilege they wore on their heads like Sunday hats. Our prose grew more and more heavy, until not only would it not break, but it turned immovable, like a bronze statue in a park. Who that man was mattered to us, but how we transposed him into words did not. They rained on us like rubber bullets. Our parkas frayed and fell apart, fabric scattering like feathers the dog tore up. One man grabbed a woman's ass, while another raped her. According to a spokesman, the (first) one who admitted it was guilty, and the (second) one who did not wasn't. Words hang like donuts on a president's finger as he jabs the air. Turned out he was lying, but we couldn't decide how much that mattered to us. The men I love are good men, but they're fragile. How to reach out with all the delicacy I can muster and pull them down from their perches, or out from under their beds. What are the words I need to use that are light as air and cleansed of judgment? How can I make the word true again? After his uncle's stepson killed himself on veteran's day and a girl fell to her death outside the restaurant where he edited a poem, he told us he was broken. A crushed glass is sometimes truer in the light than one that still sits on the shelf.

~19 November 2017

21

I want to write an honest sentence. My friend says no one dies while she meditates. My dog hunts drops of rain from the trees, digs claws in the dirt where they fall. Drum drops hit outside sliding glass in the room my son returns to. The ginger and white cat is on patrol. Early music upstairs, after Mozart (and before). Is survival a form of healing? he asks; if we keep it small, like the pulsing of a truck in reverse, sound shielding us from harm. It takes resources to find silence, costs extra to sit in the airport lounge away from loud announcements. Destination is at once fact and aspiration. We asked ourselves what attention is, knowing it mostly from its absence. "You learn to attend to the world, both as it is and as you want it to be," I wrote in what was called a "descriptor." Only later did he find that he'd "made women feel badly," using the adverb to compensate for a deep well of boundary crossings. Yellow tape runs between trees so you don't confuse this with "sex panic" or with dating young women because they are so "pure." How do you describe a lie so visible we can run it into a reef and watch it rust? It's a boundary we can't see but trips us up, gashing a hole in the bow and paralyzing city government, which can't seem to unstick it from the ever-bleaching coral. Since his major depression ended, he finds it nearly impossible to concentrate on anything other than audio equipment. We finished the book that argued against willpower, but still use that language. One side of the sponge was soft, the other Calvinist. The mold we scrape up can save us, if we're not allergic to it. One young man can only drink tea if it's served without leaves, and another turns it down cold. What we take as truth is a see-through wall, designed to beautify a boundary we cannot feel. He heard "the handmaid's tale" as "the hand made tail" and we laughed. It's a dark time, but if we sit on a pillow on a bench beside a tree-choked ravine where chickens cry half the night, no one will die. Promise.

~24 November 2017

I want to write an honest sentence. *I don't want to exist*, he said. To want not to be: two positives and a negative. Negative wins, masquerading as member of a team clutching its trophy for the cameras. Digital immortality is brief, though it comes around like days of the week. He sat down to draw a Valentine; what flashed before him was a sketch of himself ascending to heaven. At least there were wings. That was before the image of him lying in the tub, covered in blood. We pay attention to the film more than to the screen on which it dances. The film pierces us with need. His son's ideation involved using his friend's gun at a shooting range. *If our father could do it, so can I,* one woman reported, having lost both father and brother. It's not something we commit, except to other's memories. Her friend, dead these 20 years, still appears in her dreams, telling jokes. Ithi stands by Starbucks with Rawi, each clutching a large bag. Suicide is a stay to time, its straight jacket. At the end of *Poetry: Shi,* the audience sat quietly in the dark theater, as if to take in the braid of dementia and self-murder. Outside it was sunny and the Pacific Ocean was turquoise and people were drinking coffee and shopping. Everything as it had been. The death toll is a bell that rings for thee, and thee. A verb and its negative are the enjambment that breaks statement into counter-statement, a moment of being into one of ceasing to exist. "The horses are" was Plath's best line, my teacher said. I'm afraid to see what came next. And he is and they are yet. I feel cleaner now, he says, having told us the story of a grandfather who liked little boys. To hear is to take on but some of the weight, and to carry it away. The road's shoulders bear the strain of wanderers, men and women who walk. (To walk is to place one foot before the other, and the other after.) You can see it in their eyes, the unsettled stare. Theo wondered if our colleague had died by suicide but I said no, he was quite happy. His last glance resembled one.

--24 December 2017

I want to write an honest sentence. A saw cuts my thought in half, though both ends show outside the box. Thought's an appendage, but what occurs inside the box is not. *Is not* is assertion and denial in two short syllables. The saw would cut them in half, leaving a pile of light brown dust. What feeds the trees in the rain forest is the dust from Mongolian deserts; what feeds the dust is another question. I see from one side of the box, and wiggle my toes at the other. If sawdust makes me sneeze, I perhaps will die of being cut. But to read the box as meaningful is to take it as central to the story, succumbing to the saw. Once upon a time there was a box. Once upon a time it sat upon a stage and people watched as it was cut in half. The piercing of the saw was not entertainment but something more precious. It was what happened while not happening, this separation of the box from itself. The box is a turtle shell that shields beings from consequence. Head cannot think its way inside the box to cradle heart and liver, ease the pain of seeming to be cut. Death would be a poor performance, but life is not. The handmaid saw a sheet that wore a tulip stain of blood and knew a man had died. The other sheets were blank, like petticoats lacking ink.

~26 December 2017

I want to write an honest sentence. A heart unfolds red petals beneath little green bananas. Lacking paper, they wrote their names on banana leaves. Where now cactus is canvas for graffiti. Two letters in a row, but I can't get them right except by adding and then pruning back. My daughter spells Lord with an "a," as if he boarded with us, mystery man in the extra room. I want to say "insurance," but that's not it. Insulation is, to keep in the warm and out the cold. The law of syllables doesn't apply, though that of initial sounds seems to. The tip of the tongue resides inside the skull, where someone cracked a door. Inured to our losses, we dropped the plan, leaving higher premiums to the sick and elderly. A bearded homeless man at the bus stop on Kamehameha tilts his head down against the rain. In the suburbs, there you slink past the house of the man who molests you. So many years later, you tell the story. It fell upon your screen, but screen disappeared like a blind assassin. You'd kill your past, if you could. Instead, you gather letters like leaves and lay them on the floor. They can't grow, but you summons the wind. *I'm so glad you never played the victim.*

–28 December 2017

I want to write an honest sentence. Forgiveness is arbitrary, but the arbitrary is not. The one time the old man came to him in a dream, he was lost and confused. The sun kept rising and setting behind him. *Go into the light*, the younger man said, and he did. *Take your trauma and run it in fast-forward until it's funny* was the worst piece of advice. The best was to tell stories, but he couldn't remember in what order they fell, and they do. What was the relationship between trauma and the ordinary world? If what's ordinary is sacred, what of moments torn from its rib, given half-life and an apple for the teacher? If not sacred, then rimmed by a migraine's aura. When she reads in church she cannot see the words; there's a hole in the text, or in her head. Scripture drains away in flash flood. *Why is it funny that the Noah's Ark Theme Park flooded?* my daughter asks. Our explanations fail her. The myth of a myth is perhaps a truth. Or, the president* hit a birdie and was on television to boast about it. We don't get cable any more, so his face blurred as if protected from our gaze. Witness protection, you know. We need him re-elected because otherwise ratings would plummet. He's the engine of the fake economy, one where talkers talk and fact-checkers go on holiday. Someone made the mistake of calling this paradise, so I responded in a little box. Is tropical suffering worse than that in cold climates? He should feel better, someone said of a friend, because it's so sunny out today. But this today I walk between bands of rain. If you peel the film away from the screen, and only watch the screen, your memories will turn clear as rain water. I am obsessed with my memories, but don't hold onto them. I put them in small plastic sleeves and give them away like toothbrushes or hand soap. It's what I do to forgive myself for living in this world.

~29 December 2017

I want to write an honest sentence. The blond-haired boy who comes to play with dogs shows off his walkie-talkie. In case he gets kidnapped, he says. Who would kidnap him? His mother says someone might want his new shoes and take him away. It's the middle of the year so he wonders if he's still in second grade. The drunken man in a Houston hotel told police he needed all his weapons to keep them safe, there on the 30th floor on New Year's Eve. An Iraq War vet in Iraqi Freedom cap made videos of himself playing with a yoyo. His "critiques of law enforcement" amounted to accusing a cop (he held the deputy's card to the camera) of pimping a woman with chestnut hair who only hid behind a door. His roommate gave the soon to be mowed down cops a key to the apartment.

Logical Fallacy owns a gun. Logical Fallacy sets himself upon the world to correct its errors of precision and truthfulness, because there are conspiracies afoot. What really happened was something you can't imagine, even if you believe it. Like pedophile pizza makers supporting HRC. Logical Fallacy wants to write an honest sentence, too, one so full of detail you wouldn't need a GPS or Siri. He likes his pizza with mushrooms and pepperoni, a real American. With your AK-15, there you feel free. If only the police had guns, they could defend themselves. Beating up his wife and kid didn't quite do it for Logical Fallacy any more; that was years of ordinary hassle, all the violence and making up. He was as tired as an old construction worker. So Logical Fallacy took his weapons out where people walked on sidewalks, breathing in the air and talking about their kids. He hated that they breathed. He was Bruce Willis in an elevator shaft, white guy out to save the world. They're all terrorists, even the blonds. Logical Fallacy had been taught that showing is more effective than telling, so he knocked a hole in the glass and gazed through his rifle sight. There wasn't much to see except those others breathing. He'd take care of that. By the time the cops came in, he'd have saved the world and gone to heaven. And they did.

~1 January 2018

I want to write an honest sentence. The word for emptiness in Sanskrit signifies rotten fruit (#fake definition). Looks good on the outside, but erupts over your hand when you press it. We brace ourselves for the next twitter rant, the cant that masquerades as can, a can can by the president dressed in loud feathers dancing in a cabaret of one. He requires high surfaces, a table genius on which to prance and whinny, entertain the carrot and the sugar cube before adjourning to watch reality TV. It took the reality out of it, really, these shows about ordinary people doing ordinary things that suddenly escalated into a Duchamps wet dream. Beside the urinal a woman told her grandson that *this* was the piece that had ended art. He was maybe five years old, dressed up for the museum trip, and she was tricking him up in an aesthetic code that ripped art from use value. The golden shower video may be as beautiful as Piss Christ, though one wonders. It may be real, but is it reality-based? Or the imitation of a parody of a mafia hit that is our current politics? At least Tony Soprano watched the History Channel, you know, and talked about panic attacks with the other woman that he loved. She was raped later on, while he had done nothing to prevent it, and his guilt turned him into a harder man. Murder in the woods is an art, while murder at the dump is not. Or am I a murder snob? Having no memory for narrative, I cannot piece together an argument either way. Each timeline falls to the ground like the drone at Sunset Beach that smacked into a palm tree, only to fall to the ground in many white pieces. To see without putting your body at risk is one way to do it. Another is to take the risk without seeing, because that inspires caution we leave on the sand like the blue plastic bottle a monk seal nestled herself against. Her nose was plugged with sand, her eyelids rimmed with it. The tiny head curled back toward her bulbous gray body. Hours later, she still lay inert on the beach, while another gaggle of people watched her sleep. The rainbow over her body promised something else.

~7 January 2018

I want to write an honest sentence. "I am not a racist."

~16 January 2018

I want to write an honest sentence. But even honesty goes rigid like a body on the field of battle, one arm splayed above a broken shoulder, the other hand clinging to mud. Two diplomats on horses meet in no-man's land to broker a deal. It's so much easier post-apocalypse, when there's nothing to exchange except wounded prisoners. After Cadet Bone Spur's latest tweets, the nuclear clock advances. We have an ammo box and iodine, just in case. To think about death was easier when it came more slowly, or news of it. The process is one of steeping, of dipping tea bag in hot water and watching steam become cloud become mundane revelation. He saw Jesus in his, while his friend found Satan, assuring him he'd sell his soul for money. And he did. In his Christmas letter he told us how much we'd love to be his boxers (dogs, not shorts). One was named Buddha, and the other Daisy. The earth of Volcano is fragile, like crockery yet not so solid, layers of ash and rot and moss and ponds of water after rain. Earth is not institution but it dies. Bully bulldozer takes out segments of forest to install strip mall or suburban tract house. The hardware store proclaims "True Value," but there's nothing there except tourist trinkets and monster drinks. The conspiracy is as true as you make it, because inference is more powerful than document, and far less dull. Better to tell the story of an FBI that undermines Hillary Clinton only to advance her power grab over the greatest candidate in history, or to vaunt the white supremacist as a man of the people, where people is defined as anyone who has never crossed a border. We push our toes to the line like servers, hopes focused on the box before us, which we see through the net. We cannot play without the box, we opine. I can't remember now what year Buddha died.

~25 January 2018

30

I want to write an honest sentence. When my former colleague asks if my sentiment comes from Hemingway—he of the "one true sentence"—I note the difference between "true" and "honest." A true sentence sings; an honest one interrupts. The judge, on giving the child abuser a life sentence, pronounced it "death." A life sentence comes without an end stop, but death is all period. He thinks of retirement as prelude to dying, of open time as paralysis, but it's merely a more private form of scattering. I have my mother's ashes beneath my desk, needing to get to my father's shelf in Arlington. It's a peculiar form of procrastination, this holding onto a box in which a bag in which the gray dust of a mother's substance sits. I am exiled not from her womb but from her ash. When the priest uttered the lines "ashes to ashes" in Charlottesville, Virginia in the mid-80s, I began to weep. I thought of Holly, beside me, but couldn't stop. To put my mother's ashes on a shelf is not to scatter them but to suggest they are in a book closed behind a metal door, a possible text. The color of shredded newspaper, her bones. My friend and I talk trauma at the coffee shop. I remember my mother, at five, declaring no one would ever hurt her again. It worked, for a while, that speech act. She acted in college, got an MA in Theater. She'd meant it then, she said, to my request for an apology. As if honesty merits loyalty even after term limits expire. Her last years were a scattering before ashes. There was anger and there was sweetness, but none of it seemed true. They were the flashes of light on the screen, before final chords barge in. Cords, clouds, the smudge of blue gray green above the Koʻolau in Manoa. We turn our backs to them, head to the car to drive back home.

~26 January 2018

I want to write an honest sentence about my throbbing thumbs. Opponents to be glad-handed and condescended to, like the American people on a good day. There's video of his bald head beneath an enormous combover, carrot top in an over-coat, power dreaming. Re-figure him as a boy with freckles and trauma a mile deep cut into his body as hyper-inflation, if not attention. My neighbor says she's turned off the news because there's nothing she can do. The only doing is not doing, is lying in a bean bag chair remembering a murder out of sequence, the moment of coming out of the water and saying yes, I saw urchins and fish. The memo betrays itself, acknowledges the story started with a Greek and not the report of a pee-stained mattress. You're flying across the Riviera in a two seater jet plane, circa 1957, with the prince you've seduced to get at your womanizing husband. Your name is Brigitte Bardot, and you're still alive, Wikipedia nearly sunken beneath your lovers' names. When you tell the truth, you're told it's fake news. When you rehearse your cover story, it's welcomed as fact. As FIN sits at the screen's center, neither story seems quite right to him, but you put your finger to your mouth for us. We won't tell, especially not now, when our reality B-movie clutters with nuclear alerts and white supremacists in the streets of Lawrence, Kansas. At least they're marching during a basketball game. What idiots. They've come fully armed and on foot to support the cause of their flag (not the one they'll wave, mind you). The speech gestured toward unity of a kind found when everyone agrees, whether they want to or not. Take all the words and turn them inside-out like socks until the lint makes you sneeze. Breathe in the thought of beautiful clean coal and exhale the buck twenty-five a week that will earn you a Costco membership. We thank you, good lords, for our crumbs. Forgive us our trespasses, those that come later on. For thine is the kingdom but ours a strip mine in Appalachia. There's anger in our beautiful dust.

~2 February 2018

I want to write an honest sentence about prayer. The man who gives my dog a treat pulls his phone out of a pouch. He gets up early to do devotional reading, then finds lessons to watch while walking his dog. His accent is from North Carolina (as are his gluten-free treats), but he's lived here since the 70s. I thought he worshiped the New England Patriots, what with the shirt and hat. My mother talked about Displaced Persons wandering Europe after the War. Here I worry about micro-aggressions (a soccer dad told my daughter she should breast feed because it's healthier) when people are ripped from their families by the ICE man that cometh. Mutter Courage is surrounded by disability: mute daughter, autistic son, priest with a cane. Her ability to talk and sing won't get her out of the play, no matter how displaced the playwright insists we are. Let's all be flat characters together, and do our pilgrimages on the solid stage. He says I suffer the world. To suffer is to feel pain, or to tolerate it in others. I suffer the little children; I suffer temptation. It's like the phrase, "I forget," from which we gather in the many moments we remember. To forget is to desire forgetting, not to misplace the trauma of wandering away or toward. The baby's not to be cut in two, but torn limb from limb; only the woman who cannot pull is true. The other wants her child for his inheritance. Oh, friends, the playwright was Marxist! His priest was drunk, the marriage a sham. He likes the moments of anger that boil up like blood, turning the stage red. Peter O'Toole was so bad in Macbeth that the London paper gave it a "must see." The blood was strawberry jam. Let jam be thicker than water, and water thicker than skin. I went instead to *Krapp's Last Tape* to watch bananas. If only he could have forgotten. Tape is thicker than memory, and none so kind.

--6 February 2018

I want to write an honest sentence about the end of the world. At the gym I listen to a podcast about compassion. Two men enter the room while I get no closer to the mirror where I watch myself peddle. "Then we'll do squats," one announces. "Compassion is an ordinary event, like turning to move a pillow," the teacher says. "Are you working on your calves?" asks the man whose calves are thickest. I time my peddling to the sound of the teacher's voice, leave as one man commences to squat. The film is like that. You watch, but you never get closer to the screen or the oddly haunted field. An interminably boring masterpiece, I read. Makes time seem real, even if the action is not. Meet the dogs of Chernobyl. Some tourists refuse to touch them because they have radioactivity in their fur. But they gaze back at the camera. Simon the fox wears long white hair on his narrow hips and looks at us with human eyes. It's a "stalker's paradise," the photographer says. Time doesn't pass, the teacher insists; at 80 we're still 20 and 40 and 60. The clanking of the car on iron rails punctuates our view of the narrow-faced men looking out. The color shifts to green, as actors take their allegorical places. Here there is no audience except bent poles and berms of stone. There's terror in the ordinary. An empty pool; a wrecked classroom. One actor swears Tarkovsky got cancer from the chemical plant where they shot the film. Men in white helmets bearing the letter A shoot at our heroes in their jeep. It's ruin porn with an eerie glow, an O in the dome with a blue eye beyond. Or we're inside the eye, looking further in. Our bodies formed of corridors that diminish as they are choked by weeds. Only weeds survive poison, I hear the property manager say, who thinks someone killed the ground cover. The dumpster, at least, is green. Trees are cast white or red by the camera's lens; a dog lies beside the plaque beside the sarcophogus that retains radioactive waste. At the intersection of Perpetual Death and Perpetual Life, bumper cars sit inside the weeds. Asthmatic whacker outside my window heaves up rocks. Broken toys and a rotting grand piano. Amen.

~7 February 2018

I want to write an honest sentence in which I use the real words, not the false. Not "stalker" but "guide," not "president" but "dear leader." I'm told "leader" is the wrong word, to say nothing of "dear." When my daughter reads jokes from the internet, she pauses after each one to say she doesn't get it. We have two laughs and move on. When power mocks and the power to have power mocks itself: these are different cues, set on different stages. The one is too spare, like the wall I sense before me in zen; the other too ornate, like a joke done in brocade. Wanna beef, bra? Fake news in bad translation sounds apt, where the aide without a security clearance is found to have physically abused two wives and is pronounced "an honorable man" by "the good general." I want gold behind my words, not this flimsy paper currency they fling about these days. Translate "transparency" as "mud," "constitution" as "menu," "due process" as "tunnel." The actor found a skeleton with orange hair attached. I knew he was the actor because there seemed to be no character, only a man who wandered into a pilgrimage and took naps in toxic waste. Opposite of Sean Penn, who acts the actor, bravura non-self parading his non-selflessness. This guide couldn't enter the room because his motives had to remain pure. Not like ideological purity, but like the unstained state of seeing ideology through. He was so scared he turned the wrong way and ended up in the mogul room. A bird flew past, then disappeared in thin air, if there was any. Not CGI exactly, but a gesture at it. Like the gesture that recognizes belief without succumbing to it. Is there such a thing as pure doubt? I doubt it. One always stumbles upon the rock in the river that stubs doubt's toe. Went down the rapids backwards, we did. Now ex-Director Comey tweets a view of that same river. His word was false before it came true, like a glass pyramid turned to the light, odd shaped tongue. His daughter was mute, or did she lack legs? As the film ends, she pushes glasses across a table with her eyes as our eyes take hers in. *To take in* is either to adopt (like a group of elephants an orphan) or to absorb (like a beating). It's like *suffer* or any other word that means its own othering. His favorite scenes were those of the black dog walking in the water.

--8 February 2018

35

I want to write an honest sentence about happiness. He turns on a cartoon video about our false expectations for happiness. It's the elephant in the Declaration, this pursuit of it. The boy who killed 17 students was adopted; both his adopted parents died. 44+0. He lived with a friend and loved his arsenal, his magazines. Why the president appended his tweet about mental illness to one about immigrants: the boy's name is Cruz. I tell him I got the bit about happiness and the cartoon annoys me. The students flung their arms up in the air; one pair of hands shook like autumn leaves in a fierce wind. Except it was Florida. Not again, not here, never would imagine. The negative of death is life, and life, friends, is boring. The morning's meditation is adrenaline: blood-red headlines, photographs of students in narrow files, a military vehicle, a voice that breaks like skin. We were joking that someone might be shooting up the school and then we were running and the boy behind us was bleeding. My son keeps airsoft guns out in his room; Bryant asks him to put them away. "So many dead today," he says. When I sat facing the zen center's white wall, I felt the wall; I wanted to run into the woods screaming. It's watching you, too, the teacher says, but I want to call in a bulldozer to break it down, dry wall to dust. After dark, a large truck overwhelms the rain. Out back, pigs have burrowed around the bodhi tree. A statue of Buddha sits beside the tree's fertile cleft surrounded by patches of mud. The pigs are industrious; they work hard. Lori's Waipahu students mangle Trump's tweets: the trunchion calls on the pepperoni to do his bidding. They are new immigrants, testing out new words. Between times they speak more clearly in languages I cannot hear. One says in perfect English: "Trump is a racist jackass." I'll sit to that.

~15 February 2018

36

I want to write an honest sentence about the wall. The white wall is half as high as I am, when I stand. When I sit, it fills my sight, though eyes remain at half-mast, as the teacher instructs. Flags flew at half-staff last night at the baseball game for those dead in a Florida school. We parcel out our enemies, victims, and heroes as if. The wall makes me want to run into the hills, screaming. The teacher tells me to breathe it in; it's not really a wall. But I want to pound it with my fists, knock it into the lap of a woman sitting on the other side. She sniffles. I sit still. The wall is fragile but immovable, like my son or mother. Sits in its whiteness staring back at me. What have I done to deserve such feeling from a wall? A small child pulls out her fists and thrashes at the air; she was I and I am she and somewhere a Beatles' song repeats itself. My friend's piano arrived, as did my poem about a rotting instrument. He figures out the cost as a portion of Adam Wainwright's salary. But the piano is still radioactive, even if it's lost its keys. The memory app they'll slip in our brain will take care of keys, but what of memories that begin again at their origin and don't let us pass? What I remember is often wall. I see only the undifferentiated white, the sitting prompt. My mind intends to go white, dropping impulses like grains of rice, but its blank clots. I could wail at the wall, or I could turn away, but that would break the etiquette of quiet obedient sitting still. Breaking news of a broken system only strengthens it. The deal is a wall in exchange for allowing some to remain on the other side. Our side. Can I place myself inside the wall, as if in a tiny submarine, afloat? The coral bleach, but there's no weight, a near levity to this end of the world in heat and plastic and murder. The boy who killed them was doubly orphaned. Don't explain him away, one woman writes, "he's just a murderer, that's all he is." And so was the woman who saved so many lives, whose past was a white wall. If you peered around it, you'd see she participated in genocide. We find our balance in body counts. My spine is straight and I'm counting my breaths, you damn wall.

for John Bloomberg-Rissman
~17 February 2018

I want to write an honest sentence. Somewhere in Pennsylvania, men and women embrace AR-15s, wear golden Burger King crowns as they renew their vows. A white dress signifies lack of wound, virginity in the anthropocene. The building where a massacre unfolded will be torn down, boost to the local economy. Doing and undoing participate in the same dance, making harm in order to unmake mortar, as if to replace the building were to take away its history. (My mother asked where the Bastille was, and someone pointed to the ground.) I wonder about the flowers left on H3 beside the drop. When a woman at the retirement home said none of the windows opened, another-an Englishwoman with a French name-muttered, "they don't want us committing suicide." Her name means "flower." I saw a young man on the shoulder at that spot, his eyes broken, but I can't read words written on the pole in black marker. To wound is to make blossom; the exit from an AR-15 is the size of an orange. I take this gun to be my legally wedded spouse. I take it in my bed and perform erotic feats, nuzzling it as it warms to my touch. The spawn of my gun will have trigger finger and a perpetually open mouth. It will suck my teat until I run out of magazines, then point its tiny head at me and explode. What a sicko.

~1 March 2018

I want to write an honest sentence about my dog hunting rain on the lanai. She paws at concrete, as if to dig up drops, then shakes her head after a direct hit. Two more dead this morning in central Michigan. The more I aim to digress, the closer I come to the exact point of violence, cut like an abrupt angle. Even angels avoid us now, as their wings aren't bullet proof. Make your walls of Kevlar, but keep your AR-15s. Happiness is a warm gun, though the singer's voice is just a character. Not as sincere as the man who took him as his muse, or the one who took his life. Where do we take them? To other islands, remote ones where people still play hermit? Do we carry them like luggage, stopping to feel badly about those items we failed to check off our morning list? You need a life coach to get you through this scatter, one to call each morning and cheer you up. A cheerleader appeared in my head and waved her pompoms for me; I don't like cheerleading, but I did her, even in pink. My friend writes about angels, and I'm glad he does because someone needs to let them in the screen door to entertain us. A brush of wings and I'm aware my dog wants to hunt them, all apart from the Fed Ex package they leave by the door. A father screams that his daughter was "hunted" by the boy. The amendment is for hunters; semi-automatics are great for hunting frogs. My dog ended up at Feather & Fur after catching a toad. They washed her mouth out for an hour. A neighbor's dog died of it. When I got to class that day in south London (one man recognized accents street by street by street), they looked at me, the lone American. No, I hadn't heard.

--2 March 2018

39

I want to write an honest sentence. There was a week when I realized my life was populated nearly as much by the dead as by the living. It was a week of crossing from abstraction into decay. Memory, like entropy, is either too little or too much, or both huddled in the cloak of the other. There was always the element of surprise. Most included denial, hence the shadow of a bearded man holding a cigar that passed across the television screen—not the corrupt lawyer on a Manhattan street, but the Viennese father of another mafia. His indexes were sheer entertainment: look up "pulled tooth"! Look up "dream of swimming!" They're more forward-looking now, because what's done is done and all you can do is watch videos about how happiness isn't guaranteed, a kind of Khan Academy for the Soul. When I said I knew that, he gave me hand-outs instead, under the guise that I prefer words to images, my own voice in my own head rather than that of a cartoon character dancing on a computer screen. The apothecary shop in Hannibal, Missouri had the best name, I thought. He lifted me above the steamboat's turning wheel and I saw water falling from blade to blade. We'll keep Twain out of it, my friend said, because he takes up so much room. But no tourist was cursed for taking Twain curios from the shops, or because she read his essays from a passing ship. The extent to which that "I" is myself I can't fathom, except to say it's not projected on a Trump hotel like accusations of corruption, but ripens in my cranium (vocabulary word of the other day). Half-lives or three-quarter lives or the lives that come to meet you on the "more is more" plan, then after a few days home, disappear. It was a painless death, we're told. Or, he spent years suffering, but never complained. Or, she never told her old friends because she didn't want them to worry (was that it?) Whatever it was, narrative cracked like an egg and yolk ran red across a black frying pan, day after day, until we noted a fixed pattern of astonishment. I will sit down to write my cards to loved ones, aching to make voluntary what I already set down beside the road. They call that a shoulder. The old woman carried her shoulders like a thick ice pack; my dog ran to her and lifted brown eyes up. She leaned to pet the dog. "Sad poppet," Marthe said, when Lilith lay down beside her. Grief's puppets bow to gravity, and this stage.

~17 April 2018

40

I want to write an honest sentence. I cannot seem to write any, which is not to say they would not be true, rather concede to the exhaustion of taking it in, nasty words and more simple needs. I argued against truth, thinking it too grand, preferring in its stead some notion of poetry as a tennis racket punching each lie away at the net. My students do not understand the fiction-as-a-higher truth idea, preferring non-fiction. All ideas in facts. Fake news is fiction, but what is fact but inverse fake, some way the novel gets turned inside out like a sock, becomes the narrative of a real person seeking out real facts in a real book on a real shelf. If truth is beauty, what are facts? The highest rate of rainfall ever, turning highways into rivers and hillsides into mud puddles. The beauty of these facts is abstract. That might be the rice in the salt shaker, absorbing damp, out of commission in the starch department. A Fox host thanked the president for bringing the apocalypse closer, and this morning's news from Jerusalem might bear her out. There's no clean break in history, just vents spilling poison over the landscape. One commenter noted that Pele is reclaiming the land for Kanaka Maoli, and who's to disagree when meaning is as up in the air as a lava bomb at the highest point of its trajectory? Who's got the claim on "magical thinking" and who on "actual fact"? Men's voices approach through rain's remainder and crease of bird song. Yesterday, a white crab cartwheeled into the ocean. Today there will be more violence. *Evanescence* is too soft a word for what this world offers. It breaks us. Only if we're lucky is there glue at Longs and enough pieces left to angle together as if one is a number we could ever get to again. There's too much history between then and future then, lapsing into the tense that is not present, nor any other that we know. No electrical gadget gainsays its wobble, tunes us in.

~14 May 2018

I want to write an honest sentence. A man in Gaza swings his tennis racket at a canister of tear gas.

-15 May 2018

I want to write an honest sentence. I was or was not at the Trump tower meeting and I did or did not agree to receive incriminating evidence. I heard and did not hear the shama thrush at one distance, an ambulance at the other. I watched and did not watch a man scream at a Muslim woman. They were killed, are being killed, someone kills them at the border. Lust for fixity, for an anti-ocean, paved expanse where water has been. We sit to watch a white screen, but it's still populated by terrorists and aliens and conspiracy theories. Abraham Zapruder films the screen, but all he sees is lava spatter from a president's head, as if natural violence matched the force of a rifle's bullet. He says he's measured the toxicity of his anger and means to flush it out, but it falls like ash on Pahala, on Punalu`u, on South Point. *You must forgive* comes without an instruction manual. Her civil defense brochures sit at angles in front of a vase of flowers. That's documentation for you, with an aesthetic grace note. He infused Versailles' ponds with perfume, as if to bring another century forward, back. What we smell makes us sad, he says. For me, it's cat piss, the stink of our late cats in the stink of our present. Memory is also smell, insubstantial, unanchored to this earth, wind's intricate chances taken. Photo of an offering to Pele, ti leaves bound in a circle, pohaku at the center. Without a name, it's just a mountain. With one, it's the ethical destruction of a desecrated place. The man without legs who slung rocks at Israeli forces was shot dead yesterday. Maged reminds us he had a name. A UN soldier ducks as a sniper's bullet lands beside her. "Tone deaf murderers" suggests that somewhere there's perfect pitch.

~16 May 2018

I want to write an honest sentence. Ash is general over Ka`u. The therapist advises my husband to imagine he's holding a scalding pot, then to drop it on the floor. She imagines letting go of the blanket around her shoulders. All we have is an invisibility cloak, especially if we're older women; it's like an ID to a national park of pure observation. Mike signed my husband's name and Marthe shared my middle, inherited from my mother. In the Alzheimer's home she shed her maternity, became Martha with no-last-name. She was our child or our pet. The dog is about as smart as a toddler, cannot find her toy through the back slats of a chair. The front is still open, but she stays at the back, pawing spaces between slats, wanting to make the toy squeak with her nose. He says no one understands depression who has not lived there. Laughs at the dog, holding down his end of the rope, its many colors torn by her teeth. One man was said to turn his hose on the lava to slow it down. An old photo shows the US military bombing a flow to alter its route. It's the way men try to calm women down. Graffiti in Makiki claims Pele's ridding the island of "haoles and n—ers." Now there's a logical statement. No sentence quite refuses meaning, so we hold onto its handles like old women in slick bathtubs, hoping not to crack our bones on the way out. We'll hold onto anything, you see, to bear our mortality. My mother was afraid the doctor had bad news, was reassured it was another woman's husband who died in surgery. That was before he and she died, and Paul and Monica and Marthe and those who protested at the fence and those who answered cell phones in their back yards and those who ran away and those who stayed put. No air, he said. No air, Pele ordains, that is not ash-full. So hard to see through. I wanted to write an honest sentence about Tommy Pham, whose eyesight degenerates even as he hits over .300. He vents at the Cardinals, who kept him down so long. We love Tommy Pham for his beauty and his disgust. Marthe's twitter rage machine has come to life again. Laura reels at this new manner of grieving the dead who speak to us from our devices. "Are you driving?" mine asks, and I press "no."

for Mike and Laura and i.m. Marthe
~17 May 2018

I want to write an honest sentence about the photo of an empty chair to the other side of a dark wooden table. The viewer sees a bowl of cereal and a spoon, its handle set to the right of an avocado green bowl, thick white mug of black coffee (half full) between bowl, place mat of mixed colors, and empty chair. Beside the place setting opposite a mussed up cloth napkin. Windows behind the empty chair are blank in early light, a barely visible tree trunk more resembling falling tears than bark. Bryant picked up a thread of Pele's hair from a bed of moss, placed it on his palm beneath his ring. Ring dwarfs hair. One end of the thread is bright silver, the other a tear above a tail of curling black ash. It resembles a tiny hockey stick. His bicycle tires kick up volcanic grit, and the air smells of sulfur. He turned on a video of fissure 20 just as the bed started to shake. Arrived at Volcano golf course when the first explosion happened. His photo comes after the second boom, gray cloud trailing steam. The sky is otherwise blue and clear. Puna's coastal road was closed last night. Lava has reached the sea, sending up clouds of toxic steam. Remember when we walked past the end of Chain of Craters road, molten red flowing into deep blue water, and whales blew columns into air?

~20 May 2018

I want to write an honest sentence. I gave each old woman a flower and asked her to describe it without using the words "beautiful" or "gorgeous" or "nice" or "pretty." *It's so pretty*, they said. *So beautiful.* "She won't let us use those words!" There were lavender petals and dots. What color are the dots? There were long stems. How long? 20 inches, they wrote. Are they all green? Mostly they recognized the flower as described. I asked them to express an emotion by adding to their descriptions, but without using those words. An Englishwoman named Fleur (*how do you know who I am?* "Because you cam to my last workshop") erupted with the story of her homeless brother and their mother killed by a drunk driver, all having something to do with a yellow chrysanthemum (though she didn't remember which flower she'd started with, it might have been purple) and by that time I had given up getting them to WCW's "The Great Figure"--the poet's insertion of the word "tense"--but I shared it with them anyway. *I feel anxious about my children when I hear a siren,* one woman said. So it's you and not the truck! As I looked at them, they were pulling their flowers and stems closer, holding them to the light.

--21 May 2018

46

I want to write an honest sentence. A small salmon-colored poodle ran toward me and my dog, off her leash. I picked her up, returned her to the address on her tag. A little girl, held in her mother's arms, had tears on her cheeks. When the doctor asked about the first time I felt depressed, I remembered a stuffed animal left in a Little Rock motel. I told her my last doctor said I had a 99% chance of relapse, to which she responded it was higher than that. I cannot listen to the audio of children crying from their cages, though I do respond to a woman I don't know who wishes the mothers would simply do the right thing, go to the legal portal. Trump uses the phrase "separate but equal" in reference to his space army, but not in relation to relatives torn from their children, because of course we are not a nation of migrant camps. They might not all be relatives, even if they cry. I love letters, but I detest the letter of the law. Besides, the photographs are old. If there is evidence we deny it; if there is none, we invent it. An older man in dreadlocks sits in the park where my son plays baseball; on the other side of a rock wall a middle-aged couple sets up their tent on a sidewalk. I offer them toiletries, catching sight of a container of Q-tips as I hand over the plastic bag. The better to hear traffic as it streams by their tent. My interlocutor points out that there are homeless children in our country, as if that mitigates those who arrive at the border with their mothers. Their homes shall be tents or chained link cages. They shall be flown to other states in airplanes, wearing Walmart goods and numbers. No one shall hug them, neither flight attendant nor sibling nor congressman nor judge. No one will clean their ears, or wash their faces or brush their teeth. They shall be our ransom and our goad. A small child surrounded by official knees cries. There is no poodle in the photograph. Nor is there a mother.

~19 June 2018

47

I want to write an honest sentence. A dream of pink bodies on the beach spliced with one of dead brown children. Pull your focus in, three monk seals dead of what cat shit contains. Bryant says he hates to kill roaches. Time is an engine, but Belgium's a damn freight train. That was not a traditional head butt, the announcer opines of the Colombian player on the line. When the bereaved party tells her story, you must not include judgment in your mirroring. We have confiscated your words at the border, shrink-wrapped them to avoid damage. An undamaged word floats in a no-gravity space, cannot find its sentence even as it dreams of bridges and forests and a GPS so powerful it creates the landscape while miming it. We've lowered the warning levels, though each hour packages several small earthquakes that lead to a larger one, house shaking like a boat at dock. You get your land legs back by flying to another island. There are birds here, too, and morning rain that makes the dog limp and tired. A naked pink doll sits beside a red trike on our walk and I don't have my phone to take it. I am ardently civil to the pot-bellied man who walks the one-eyed dog and calls himself a lonely centrist. He hates Trump, but he loathes Hillary more. Told me I fit in at the university with all those leftists. The mail carrier in pith helmet mutters about my long vacation, and I'm tempted to leave him my resume, but who the hell cares. He plays the market, goes to Vegas to take classes, talks your ear off about how to make money. I like him, too. The door opens, I'm typing, and Bryant asks if I'm writing.

~3 July 2018

I want to write an honest sentence. A helicopter stitches the mountain, disappearing into its creases, emerging through mist. A round headlight flickers on and off. We can hear it, though we don't know its errand: errant hiker, downed line, plant survey. If you see someone hanging from a cable, you know. Power cables mimic the mountain's lines in cloud. My dog tries to play with a gap-toothed gardener who reaches in thick gloves for his rake. When I say I want to be a Buddhist chaplain, my kids tell me I'm too angry. The TV keeps me ginned up, even as gin pins me to the couch. Trump's private audience with Putin is planned without interpreter or notes. Nothing there! When I write that I admire Adnan's meditations, Norman responds that no American could hold such a large view. To make one's world small is characteristic of men who've been abused as children; getting out in the world is what spurs anxiety, chaotic word spill, nerve drills. She has to move her neck when she plays soccer, the blood flow is so strong. But that's something else. It's all something else, this sewing of lines or limes—Marthe makes mother into lime and, while her ending doesn't quite work, the acid image does. My mother Martha hated herself for hating her mother screaming hysterically in the dark, as I screamed after my father's heart attack. We try so hard to forgive the dead, to love ourselves as mothers. Trauma travels generations, a friend says, his son's great grandfather an opium addict, his son a bit lost. Another grandfather watched his sleeping grandson through the window—and that was the least of it.

—5 July 2018

I want to write an honest sentence. An empire dissolves in an acid bath of lies; I dip my foot in vinegar to kill a fungus that lives between my third and fourth toes. It likes a basic environment, Bryant tells me. The president manufactures a violent pity, piety matched to a sacred gun. Go fund the little girl's surgery, the man's rehab, redeem the coupons of our anguish. A psychopath's self-study guide would include questions about intent, the ardor required to carry it out. Pity without empathy is all self-directed.

My dog pushes up on my hands when I meditate. She licks my leg when I type. She turns her big brown eyes at the precise angle to touch me. She places her head between her two front paws: one side clear claws, the other side black, her ears up like satellite dishes. She dishes out the self-pity, wanting a walk.

Wind rustles in the near palm, the further trees. Birds chitter in layers. The earthquake map spills outward from the summit in yellow and red dots. House like a hammock in the wind. The outcome is either 1) very good; 2) very bad; or 3) takes the middle way, whatever that way is.

The dog has moved beside my chair. She stares at my feet. A woman climbed under the Statue of Liberty's foot, as if to be ground down by her heel or to persuade her of something. Suffer the little children in a court of law, testifying at age three about their missing mothers, their missing brothers. Suffer, the president says. That's how he negotiates. That's how he negates.

How do you write, my former teacher asks. How do you read, one might ask in return. Do you take what is crafted and drill a hole in its hull? Do you take its material and de-matter it? Is meaning immaterial before it enters the bloodstream, like lead? If I were in Flint, he says, I'd kill someone. Hard Flint. The man who studied psychopaths was one. He only lacked the urge to kill.

Adulthood is a suburb we inhabit only to the extent that we accept its boundaries. The small lot begins from stone, ends in soft earth that easily shifts. The earth is so fragile I want to bend down and hold it still.

for Alfred Corn
~8 July 2018

I want to write an honest sentence; rather, I want to write a not dishonest one. The double negative gives me an out, for that is what I hadn't not intended to say. ALL CAPS HELP MAKE THE POINT MORE PRECISE, like sharpening a pencil with an air hammer. Our country has jumped the shark: that reference comes from a sitcom; that is also relevant. The depressed people on the video used abstract language only. She was worried that it was getting worse. He was terrified of something about to happen. There was a forest where you couldn't hear a tree fall because there were no trees. No bark, no birds, nothing but the rustling of plastic refuse below the idea of a canopy. Leaves are the history of that idea. The house that contains them is smaller on the outside than within, a cinched belt that leaves small trails of dust down each corridor and before the toilet she sat on during the missile alert, contemplating her end. Where oh where have the nouns gone that got us here, the rich ones with lots of letters, lining up like squares of chocolate at a pot luck? When I curl my shoulders forward and put my chin to my chest, I am that girl again, the one who said "space waste" in lieu of how she felt. It's a kind of dementia, depression, displacing truth with metaphor, metaphor with blurts of sound. Air raid sirens didn't go off that day, a first clue. Still, we considered last words when only dust would become of us. Post-trauma, we're reborn as someone who just resembles us. As Sangha and I entered the hospital elevator, a tiny baby was wheeled out on a cart. A local man, tattooed, looked at me and said, "that was the scariest drive I ever took, 10 miles an hour." After the phone call about where to put the car in case of nuclear attack, they hung up and screamed. Shoshona Felman said she sent the right letter to the wrong address. It had something to do with Lacan. Later, Sangha asked about *our* first drive. I sat in the car, while the others bought formula; a land mine survivor approached with a smile and a bowl. I didn't tell him that.

~23 July 2018

I want to write an honest sentence. Once upon a time a mother duck adopted 76 ducklings. She put them all in row, of course, just as I've come up with two sore thumbs, sticking out like puffy masts from the frigates of my hands. To tell the honest truth, I never thought it'd come to this, lies buried as deep as Troy and heretofore as hidden as the horse. Only the naked and the dead are true, though the bearded man who pisses in the sea could be said to have evaded that rule. I'd thought he'd identify with Hannah in Nanette, but instead he took the part of the straight white man. His anger kept me awake at night; hers kept him. Pretend you're holding a scalding object and drop it on the ground. Pretend the ground is solid ice. But back to the drop; it eases the pain of your burning hand, the one that stands in for your heart. The peach is an ambiguous symbol, as the girl is left to carry her pit from the scene of the crime. We eat our accusers like the goat at the petting zoo who took the boy's map. It comes back as a multi-colored globe. The novel has a protagonist who listens, known only by her name. As she transcribes, her ears grow larger and larger until they resemble the goat's enclosure, path around a small island populated by rocks and short grass. One goat sits behind a sign that cautions against touching it. A stress-free zone. I tell him the point of the monologue was to disown anger, to ease the tension by refusing to create it. But she did. On that stage, the dyke Lear lamented all those who'd betrayed her. Not daughters, men. Two rapes and an attack. First as farce, then as crime. I spilled two cups of water on my bare feet, then nearly ran into a sergeant in uniform in the parking lot. She in her white car, I in mine. I had slipped my troubled teen on like a cape, but thumbs couldn't undo the tie around my neck. To hang oneself is an act of anger, she said, as someone has to cut you down. But there's always discovery; the edge of *that* continent was as sharp as a knife. Call a dead woman by her name, the land by its.

~26 July 2018

53

I want to write an honest sentence. The difference between an order and a should construction is likely a matter of timing. In the Sessions of sweet silent thought the attorney general will be canned, his deputy sent out to pasture. A cow mooed this morning, a clock ticks; as I walked up the hill, I heard an earthquake in the groaning of the nearest house. My friend could call them to the decimal point before she stopped noticing. The house is a boat, anchored on porous earth. 'Ohi'a trees stand, not yet victims of the virus; coqui frogs chant a mile away, but not here, and the air is only sometimes acid. A violet belt of vog weaves through the Saddle, and where the horizon was is now a pastel smudge. It's not what we can't see that disturbs us, but that we see it laid out before us. He reached for the tortoise, but its legs were boiling away. A little girl died in ICE custody. They're summer camps, the president says, horrified his campaign director was put in solitary. They were all screaming obscenities, but we see her in a bubble, the blonde woman whose third finger thrusts forward at the reporter, face tangled, body coiled. She and they are making America great again. We could state the obvious in perpetuity, but where would it get us? To the next station of what cross? I wondered what the X meant in Charing X Road. The pope puts a cardinal in solitary to work on penance, which sounds like what he showed his altar boys. Sound unsenses us. Get as close as you can to the aching beams and the crickets. Cut out the middlemen, the lobbyists of meaning, the men in ostrich coats. Ostracize the priests, the grandfathers, the kind man across the street, the military baby-sitter, the perverted customs agent. I have put a good face on it, my friend says, but I am so disillusioned, so tired. As the Buddhists say, we are softened. Marvel at those who remain so solid on their solid earth.

for Carla Billiteri
~1 August 2018

I want to write an honest sentence. Start again from the so-called "prompt'; the age demands speed, but ordains surface complexity. All you need know is contained in Manafort's ostrich coat. An ostrich sprints down an Australian road, while professional goats eat up Boise's flowers. They are browsers, not grazers, my son's girlfriend says, chuckling at the company that promises well-cut lawns. What it means to grow old. What it means to be on the downside of the arch in a tub, having peered through portholes at a city that promises an opening for us white folks. How easily information turns to judgment, judgment to hectoring. Who can tell the hurricane from the volcanic "event"? Do I send him black sand and lava rock, despite Pele or a park ranger's mythological purchase? My book on ethics sits in the shed, softening in the humid air. The man in ostrich coat hid income on his taxes. "Our houses are worth nothing now. Should we pay?" To which the man from the county said, "Yes, we're still collecting." What it means to pay, or pay off, to offer a defense so flimsy it demands a pardon. What it means to grow old at such a time, when earth casts off her coat and magma fills 300,000 Olympic-size pools (for those of you not familiar with scientific lingo). To lose one's "brother" or one's wife. Or, in depression, to lose what is not there but feels lost, the threat of a lava tube below the surface of one of three highways across the island. One woman asked and asked again who would watch for her kids who play on the emergency by-pass road. My neighbor leaned over, whispering, "she should tell her kids not to play there." Sun through the front windows, mist to the side, earth stumbles underneath. Time lapses like the crater spilling rock (deeper than the Empire State Building). We compare these events to objects, somewhere on the road to the volcano where the invasive species have settled. The air breathes their perfume. When the wind shifts, it'll be sulfur dioxide.

~3 August 2018

I want to write an honest sentence. Interrupted, she said she lives alone with her cats, speaks whenever she feels like it. Laughter precludes apology. Yes, there was a meeting, but results were disappointing, and besides nothing was illegal. Who's to know which statement is true, the one we suspect, or the one we wish for? They're all sentences, or most of them, carrying bare minimum of verb and noun toward a moment of confusion or collusion. Change the word to "conspiracy." Or "piracy." The earthquakes stopped; a day later and apropos of nothing, my bedside lamp fell to the floor. To live on an earth without intention is to suffer. We could demand that Pele apologize, but the Christians down Highway 11 have declared her "fake news." She at least intends, though what we cannot know. What I love about the teachings is their being drenched in metaphor; we talk not about yearning, but about potato chips. Those who were adopted live inside the metaphors the rest of you weave. It's a mythological condition, loss and recovery acted out by the village clown. It was everything I'd read all these years, staged before me, except the stage was also real. The eyes of the elders gazed at me through narrow, lined faces. I drank my tea from a glass and gazed back. The meeting was about adoptions, and then it was about dirt.

for John Gallaher
~6 August 2018

I want to write an honest sentence. Humility has to do with the soil, my neighbor tells his son. To be soiled is another thing. We draw in the word "dignity" only to dignify our choices: the retirement home radiates the word in its tables and chairs. There's nothing plastic about dignity. I refuse to dignify his tweet about lowlifes and low IQs; he's at the level of humility, but not playing it well. Shit might be the better word, its clean crisp sound. He said my poem seemed more finished than most, which meant that it had ended, like the final "t" sound of lock on a shed door. She cannot bear to take her lover's toothbrush out of their cup. He takes pictures of his empty house. She describes her dreams, gets her telephone number right, but he's gone, nonetheless. I would like to see a decent country again before I die, the poet writes to me. On the eve of my 60th, I think about death and country, numbers and tooth brushes. Nothing seems trivial, or all. The printer reads "brother"; the dog under my bed snores. There will be no secret recordings. The distinction between pain and suffering is worth noting; suffering is pain after you think about it. To render hurt into language is to suffer from it. It is hurt, but it is also sound. Sound clots like blood where the wisdom tooth was. Patrick Wisdom got his first major league hit. Wisdom is the ribbon at the end of the race; we cut through it with our flailing bodies. When I dreamed in French, I couldn't speak it, but everyone else's trilled. I was at the grocery store counter, trying to buy my goods. The air smelled of grilled chestnuts and the film ended in super slow motion.

~13 August 2018

I want to write an honest sentence. In case you missed it, you can't believe the intelligence community because they're serial killers and you can't believe the president because he's a lying narcissist and you can't believe the media because they need ratings and you can't believe your spouse because he's been abused and you can't believe your kids because they're teens and you can't believe yourself because who are you to judge and you can't believe your students because they want good grades and you can't believe the airport van driver because he wants a tip and you can't believe in kindness because it's false and you can't believe in meanness because it's true and you can't believe in God because he's so last millennium and you can't believe in celebrity because what did they ever do except sing a few songs and you can't believe Aretha because she's dead and you can't believe Miles Davis because he was improvising and you can't believe poetry because there's cultural capital to be made and you can't believe your editor because he wants to publish your book and you can't believe anyone likes your work because they'd say so anyway and you can't believe you fit in because you don't (*who IS that damn haole woman?*) and you can't believe your animals because they want to be fed and you can't believe your car because it breaks down and you can't believe in tariffs because they kill the economy and you can't believe in the economy because it's rigged and you can't believe in rigged witch hunts because they're, well, rigged and you can't believe in tweets because they're too short and you can't believe in social media complaints about the school because it does have resources and you can't believe in resources because someone wants to be in charge of them and you can't believe in authority because it's abused and you can't believe in abusers because they leave holes in your soul and you can't believe in your soul because the hole grows every year like the plastic patch and you can't believe the television anchor just burst into tears because her children go to Catholic school and the man she's interviewing says he was abused and you can't believe the priest had him drive the car when he was ten so he could fondle his genitals and you can't believe any of it. I climbed the stairs with the dog yesterday to see an old man in a cap drag one bad leg, while in his right hand he clutched red roses in clear plastic.

~16 August 2018

I want to write an honest sentence. My son leaves to do an honest day's work, while I stay home to write sentences. The television splits its screen between two dumb-faced courthouses. After a verdict, a woman in a blue dress sprints away from one of them. We talk about persuading those who will not be persuaded. It's not logic we reach for, but a counter-emotion to fear. The man who took beautiful photos of our kids at the pool claimed Clinton's henchmen called him every night to threaten his life. (I wrote "lie.") A former student thought there was a bug in his penis, installed by the government. Paranoia requires system, or is it the other way? Do not disturb the toothbrush in the cup or the place-setting at dinner. They are as they should be present. We assume the air, the trade wind through the palm with one dead frond, the round pot our dog digs in, fledgling bird songs, an entire world free of twitter and white nationalism. It no longer seems macabre to imagine my own death, but brute anticipation of fact. My dog pokes his nose into the white cat's side. He's the cat who's 14 on one block and four on the next, the one who comes when you call him. Orange splotch on his narrow white face, above pellucid blue eyes. I pause to watch, scratch the cat, then turn up the hill with my dog.

~22 August 2018

I want to write an honest sentence. We bathe us in our blood money, covering arms and shoulders with it, bearing it down stairs to join our families, seated on their blood-red couches. Everyone was so relaxed, wiping blood off their plates, their forks, their teeth. Her smile beamed red until gravity changed its hue. The house fits; no corner outgrows itself into dim and unannounced hallways. There are no rats, no mice, hardly any roaches to drink from puddles, carry the thick substance in sippy cups to their young. Despite the blood, floors are clean, walls hung with over-familiar paintings. In one, a girl seems to writhe on the bed, a cat's fur stretched like orange taffy until it blurs. "Many victims feel this way." The scent of the old man's breath inhabits the stuffed chair he sat in. Great pretender. In a dream, he comes to ask where he should go and is sent away for good; but still he comes back, holding the promise of suicide on his palm, the lure of self-hate. He was a very careful man for whom they care even in his death. What dreams his ashes have at the top of the ridge near the bunkers, finally able to fly from the broken need of his blood. The other will be a stronger man for this, I'm told, his pale face filling with color as he reorganizes his memories in a bank. But how can he reclaim his blood, and where to put it inside? There's a broken fingernail, a sore thumb, a cut on his ankle. Hand me the siphon, the needle; let me dig in.

–24 August 2018

I want to write an honest sentence, and then I want to revise it. Not to put it in a vise and clamp it down, but place it in a different light. I saw a sea urchin shell on a rock wall, spines spilling around it. Each a black wand, at one end a white plug that sat in the skeleton's ball and socket. The philosopher saw an octopus dying, her body parts dissolving in sea water. Death is one such revision. So is breath as it runs its tunnel. Describe the feeling in your chest, the brightness in your spine, and I will say it back. "We're all going to die," Marthe said, "and no one will remember us. That's ok." The urchin is a lantern: its top is anus, and its bottom mouth. The entire body might make a compound eye. I see it through a chain link fence, and the mechanical waterfall beyond. A blaze of purple shows in my photograph.

~30 August 2018

I want to write an honest sentence and then tease it open. My doctor says her emotions are for putting in a box across the room. She didn't get poetry in her genes, she tells me, only arts and crafts. We (verb) craft or we set out to sea in our (noun) craft. The doctor makes a sound somewhere between confusion and disgust. I suggest she read a poem without that noise. What I forgot to say is that her box is a poem. The houseboat is house without tenure or the hope of tenure; there's no insurance, no pension, just one thin plank between cot and a harbor that isn't one. It's all "fake news," because words function, rather than mean. "Be careful how you respond, sir," Sen. Harris said, suggesting words might function in honest sentences. The nominee, flustered, says he doesn't know what she wants to hear. He's the good student, the boy in the bubble, the judge grown in a terrarium. Sangha's shrimp have made more shrimp under their bright light beside the flag on his wall. To kneel before it is an act of consumption. Either you consume the flag or your shoes. Nike's new ad is about being the *very* best. Let's not fool ourselves, a friend says, we're not Bodhissatvas, not even close, but we move closer with attention. The fruit of each morning's meditation is a photograph, the bright and back-lit green of a leaf with narrow threaded veins. A shower tree in front of purple clouded mountains. The sea urchin, whose spines dissolve into lava rock. My dog on the wall my children walked on. The nominee is a leaf: we see him for what he is. A weak man, terrified.

--6 September 2018

62

I want to write an honest sentence about love, but I keep confusing it with fascism. The leaders sent each other beautiful letters and then they fell in love. The rest of us live in trauma-land, white walls stenciled with flashbacks, a roller coaster ride that dips around a statue of Stalin, who hears our screams as his joy and not ours. At the soccer game I set my chair on concrete. A bright green praying mantis with one back leg hobbled between me and the woman sitting beside me. She'd been reading a text out loud about her granddaughter who can't get out of bed or comb her hair. This happened after she won an award. She's had good treatment; this has been going on for a long time. My neighbor's gentle with the mantis, letting it sit between her two legs. We miss the game's only goal because she forgets the mantis and jerks it off her leg. She apologizes. It falls on concrete, abdomen heaving, its one bad leg skittering. It hugs a metal chair support. Her grandson is a missionary in Africa. The game ends. The mantis is dying. Her friend finds a leaf of appropriate size and they cajole mantis onto leaf. Friend carries mantis to the grass beneath the tree. It'll be more comfortable on the ground in the shade. Walking to the car I see the man beside the bicycle who'd been talking loudly about dog sleds. The blizzard is coming, he'd said on a hot day when the trades had stopped. There's a golf cart beside him now. My dog sleeps under her blanket on days like this. When I put my cereal bowl down, she comes out to drink.

~2 October 2018

In the midst of our troubling American present, as we find ourselves in an accelerated drift toward intolerance, illiberalism, and the looming specter of fascism both globally and locally, Susan M. Schultz offers *I Want to Write an Honest Sentence,* her genre-defying meditation on politics, culture, and identity that brilliantly investigates the personal and the political and everything in between. In short, poetic, essayistic entries spanning the summer of 2017 to the fall of 2018, she reveals to us the power of art—in its timeless interrogation—to counter the lies, unreality, and insanity encroaching upon our everyday lives. This is a beautiful book. —Timothy Denevi

Susan M. Schultz contemplates both language's responsibilities and semantic-political opacities through this gorgeously streaming poem series, whose title phrase becomes a mantra repeatedly stating a seemingly simple desire: that the "I" "write an honest sentence." But what is the meaning of either "honest" or a "sentence" in this formally challenging prose-poetry book, when human-perceptual experience—a *language* experience—is truly as unreadable as a view of "the mountain"? From this book's "clutter" of visual images (Dorito bags, dog ears framing ocean waves) to its lapses into quotidian noise ("car alarms... digital music pulse, my daughter's voice"), Schultz rejects the falsely unified speaker of conventional poetic lyric, and its equally falsely unifying conjectures about self vs. world—as tired and worn out as today's "fake news." Schultz reasserts a feminist American poetics tradition that exposes the contingent relations to various observing "selves"—in interwoven "sentence" micro-story arrangements that offer a perfect scrutiny of our social-political realities. —Laura Hinton

"It's hard to write an honest sentence in an age where public life has reduced sincerity to a political tactic. In this collection, a prose poetry diary of a year under Trump (diaries, the privileged vehicle of honest writing), Susan M. Schultz struggles for a language that retains the redemptive power of memory and attention without denying or sidestepping the destructive force of the political real. The result is both intimately personal, an Ashbery-tinged memoir of family, trauma and the Hawaiian landscape she so palpably loves, and a jarring document of the political present. It's a work to be savored." —Adam Thurschwell